Copyright © 2016 by Joli Michelle

All rights reserved. Without limiting the rights under copyright reserved above, no part of this publication may be reproduced, stored in or introduced into a retrieval system, or transmitted in any form, or by any means (electronic, mechanical, photocopying, recording, or otherwise), without prior written consent from the copyright owner.

ISBN-13: 978-1537049137

31 DAYS OF PLEASING MY HUSBAND

By: Joli Michelle

ACKNOWLEDGEMENTS

First and foremost, I have to thank my Father God. Thank you Lord, for your grace and mercy. Your forgiveness and blessings have gotten me to where I am now. Thank you for life and giving me the ability and strength to be able to finish my 31 days. Father, thank you for restoring my marriage, and helping Dee and I with our communication towards one another. I love you Lord. Next I'd like to thank my husband. Thank you Poppa, for sticking by my side. Thank you for accepting me and my flaws and putting up with this attitude. Thanks for listening to me on all those late nights and giving me advice on the book. Thank you for showing me so much love throughout the days and making this easy, to do for you. I love you so much and I'm proud to be your wife. Thank you to my beautiful sisters, Arvie and Jordan, for all of your encouragement to finish my book. I appreciate and love you both! Arvie you've stayed up with me, cried with me, prayed with and for me, and I'll forever love your soul! I admire you so much. Thanks for being the best big sister ever. Kaybee, thank you for your guidance and all of your advice. I appreciate you and I love you. Special thanks to my red bone, Precious. Thanks so much for reading over the book and giving your input. You mean so much to me. Another special thanks to my sister from another mother, Alivia. Thanks so much Liv, for editing my book. You are truly an inspiration and I appreciate you. I love you so much and I can't wait until you have the baby so I can spoil him! Thanks to my bestie Aisha Hasina. No matter what I decide to do, you're there to have my back, and I'll forever love you for that. Special thanks to my mom and dad. Ma, you taught me how to be a good wife and mom. Thank you! I thank you both for giving me life. Thank you for being so excited for me, in everything I do. Daddy, thank you for showing me how I should be treated by men. Thank you for teaching me how to pray and to ALWAYS put God first. I love your soul. Thanks for praying for Dee and I. From good times to troubled times, you both were always there and always have our back. I love you. Thanks to my Bumble bee, one of the dopest authors in Cleveland! Ivy, thank you for giving me the information I needed. Thanks for all of your tips and advice and thank you for showing me everything that I needed to do. I'll always love you. Thanks to my chocolate delight for everything! Jeneen, you've been a sister, a mom, a friend, a bank, lol everything! Thank you for all of your advice and most of all, thank you for being my friend. I'll always

cherish our friendship. To my Christian Dior, thank you Chris for all of our talks, your advice and pushing me to finish the book as well. Your hustle and ambition has pushed me to accomplish something that I really wanted. Thanks for giving me the opportunity to be a model for your dope t shirt line, and thank you as well for being a real friend to me. I love you. Thanks to my love bug, L'Tan. Since I've met you, you've been nothing but a friend to me. Thanks for ALL of those lunches you were cooking me on my lunch breaks. They gave me life!! And thank you for all of your encouraging words and support. To my Angel, Pooh (Classie Fryer) when I first told you I was writing my book, you were so happy for me. You said how dope it was, and how I was a great wife. Thank you Pooh. May you rest in heaven. I love you and miss you. Last but not least, special thanks to my babies, Destiny and Danaya. You both put up with my busy schedule, and being patient while I wrote every other day. Mommy got yall. But yall knew that already. I love you both dearly...

CONTENTS

Day 1- The Dinner

Day 2- Massage

Day 3- Indoor Picnic

Day 4- Movie Date and Drinks

Day 5- Sunday Football

Day 6- The Amazing Grapefruit

Day 7- Coupon Booklet

Day 8- Love Note and Small Gift

Day 9- Another Woman

Day 10- Movie Night

Day 11- Gas Her Up

Day 12- Luxurious Bubble Bath

Day 13- Insurance Lady Prank

Day 14- Sextivities

Day 15- Video Game Night

Day 16- Positive Sticky Notes

Day 17- Movie of His Choice

Day 18- Sweetest Day Surprises

Day 19- A Time To Remember

Day 20- Spicing It Up

Day 21- Foot Soak and Foot Rub

Day 22- Wedding Reminder

Day 23- Desserts and Wine

Day 24- Free Style Friday

Day 25- The Jet Hanger

Day 26- Clean Out His Car

Day 27- Asian Food Night

Day 28- Game Stop

Day 29- Ice Cream Run

Day 30- Balloons of Appreciation

Day 31- The Dance

INTRO

Many women can be attention whores. I can honestly admit that I fell into that category for a moment. Of course it wasn't intentional. I just felt like I didn't get the attention and love that I needed from my husband. We weren't in a good space. I could tell we were slowly straying away from each other. We had arguments like any other married couple. But the lack of love and attention is what pushed me away. My Love Languages are "Quality Time and Physical Touch"... When I'm not getting those things then that's a problem! Dee on the other hand, his love languages are "Words of Affirmation and Acts of Service". Dee didn't have many problems with me because I fulfilled his love language needs. I compliment my husband on a regular basis. I try my best to make sure he didn't have to lift a hand at home. I fed his ego all the time! So he was fine! But me? Nah, I felt like I wasn't wanted. So when other men showed me that attention, my head got big! I'd lie if I said I didn't love it. Someone buying you lunch, telling you how gorgeous you are on a daily basis. As a woman you want to hear those things! BUT, it means more when it comes from our mates. I can now admit that it was nothing but the devil. The devil wanted me to feel like my husband didn't love me. He wanted me to be attracted to other men. He wanted me to get a divorce! I didn't realize these things then, but suddenly I woke up. I had stopped going to church like I should have been. I wasn't reading the bible how I should have. I was slipping big time! Mentally I was not in a good place. My husband and I weren't communicating how we should have. We argued about money all the time. I just didn't feel loved. We didn't see eye to eye on a lot of things. It was all bad. I just couldn't understand why we couldn't get along any more. So one day I looked at myself in the mirror and I cried. I was hurting. I wasn't myself. The only thing I thought to do was pray. I fell to the floor and I asked God to forgive me. To forgive me for allowing the devil to make me feel that way. I asked God to lead me in the right direction, to help me to forgive how he forgives and to love how he loves. I prayed to be an understanding wife. I asked God to help me submit to my husband without arguing or debating all the time. I simply asked God to fix my marriage and to help me to not worry about my husband loving me, but to show me, that HE loves me and wants the best for my marriage. I asked God to get rid of all negative thoughts and to help me make my marriage better. I prayed, I fast, and then it hit me! I got my answer! I'd show my husband how much I love and appreciate him for 31 days straight, and then maybe he'll feel loved and will show it in return. I decided to stop complaining to my husband and to stop telling him what I need from him and telling him what he doesn't do. I gave it God. Now, my book is not to tell anyone what they need to do to please their husbands. It's strictly telling you what I did for my husband and how I enjoyed pleasing him. You can go through a lot with one person, but your energy can definitely turn things around. I feel like one of our issues was that we didn't spend a lot of time together because we worked different shifts. It's now time to fix that. Tomorrow, I will start my "31 Days of Pleasing My Husband". I told myself that every day for 31 days, no matter how I feel, I will do something special for him. Something that will make him feel appreciated, loved or happy. Knowing what his love language was, made things really easy for me. We've been married for 9 years now. I'm going to add a little spice. Don't get me wrong, our sex life is amazing, but sometimes you get comfortable in your relationships and you don't feel the need to do anything extra to please your mates. It's very important to keep your mate happy and interested in you. I really hope my story gives you some type of faith. To know that whatever you go through, God will get you through it. I hope you enjoy...

My First Prayer Before I Started

Father God, first I'd like to thank you for waking me up this morning and letting me live to see another day. Thank you for giving me a kind heart and giving me this idea. Lord, I thank you for my husband and I ask that you help me to be the best wife that I can be. Father, please forgive me for the sinful things I've said and done. Anything that I've said or done that was not pleasing unto you Father, please forgive me. Please help me to love, how you love, and to forgive how you forgive. I need you Lord. I need you to make me better. Please help me to go into my 31 days with an open heart and an open mind. Please help me to resist any temptation coming my way. Please help me to keep a positive mindset throughout these 31 Days of Pleasing My Husband. I said that no matter how my husband makes me feel, I would still do something special for him throughout this time. So Lord I ask that you help me to stay motivated and kind. Please get rid of any grudges, any hurt and pain that I may have had. I am your child Lord and I ask that you help me to stay strong. Please bless me spiritually, emotionally and financially. Lord his cell phone is ALWAYS a problem to me, so please touch Dee as well and show him how to focus on me when I need him most. I love you and I thank you again Father... In Jesus name Amen.

Day 1- The Dinner

Typically my husband gets off of work at 10:30 pm. He gets home around 11:08p.m, 11:14p.m at the latest. Yes I have that down to a TEE! By the time he reaches home, I already have both of our daughters in bed and I have his dinner in the microwave. That way, he can come home, heat it up, watch ESPN and just relax. For my first day, I switched it up. I wanted Dee to come home to a sexier atmosphere. Candle lit dinners are rare in our home since we work different shifts. My husband loves when I wait up for him at night. Since we haven't been on the same page lately, that hasn't been happening, so I'm sure he'll be surprised. Especially once he sees what I have in store for him. We have a plain wooden table in our dining room. I wanted to dress it up a bit. I pulled out a nice tablecloth and put some rose petals all over it. I bought some heart shaped candle holders that held small tea light candles on the inside of them. I placed those around the table. I grabbed two of my black stoneware plates with the bowls to match and I sat them directly across from each other. For dinner I prepared stuffed shells, with some croissant shaped rolls, and a nice salad. I bought one of my favorite red wines as well, and I placed two wine glasses on each side of our plates. I dimmed the lights so he could notice the candles. The table looked amazing!! This is officially the beginning of my 31 days.

Dinner was prepared and warming in the oven, now I have to get sexxxxxaaaay. I pulled my curly hair into a pony tail and jumped in the shower. My husband LOVES my Almond and Shea butter body wash scent, so I decided to use that. I took a quick shower and put on my Almond and Shea butter body butter. Since I was going for a sexier vibe, I wanted to dress sexy as well. Typically, when Dee gets home I already have on my pajamas. Ladies, you know we love to sleep in those big comfortable t-shirts, but not tonight! I threw on some black laced boy shorts from Victoria's Secret with a black laced cami top to match. Cute, sexy and simple. I even threw on my diamond studs... Just so I wouldn't look so plain. I puckered up my lips and put on a coat of my Chanel lip gloss, a little eye liner and mascara. I'm pretty pleased by my look. I'm not conceited, just convinced. I knew Dee would be home any minute. I hurried to the kitchen and put all of the food on the dinner plates and bowls. As soon as I finished, I heard the door unlock. I looked at the time on my cell phone and it read 11:08 pm. Right as I planned!

Dee walked in the house and put his lunch bag down in the kitchen. I heard the microwave open and shut. He turned around and just knowing my husband so well, he was about to ask where's my plate. But when he saw me, his eyes lit up. Now KEEP IN MIND, we haven't been on the best of terms. So I'm sure he's wondering, "What's really going on?" He licked his lips and smiled. His dimples drove me crazy!!! He walked up to me and kissed my lips. He hugged me so tight and slouched over to lay his head on my shoulder. I hugged him back, took off his hat and rubbed his freshly shaved bald head. Hugging him I think to myself how much I love this man. To go from arguing and not speaking at all, to this hug, means a lot to me. After the hug, he just stared at me for a while. No words were spoken between us. He then kissed my lips. That kiss alone said, "I'm sorry". Then of course he asked "what's for dinner." I grabbed his hand and walked him into the dining area.

Presentation is EVERYTHING! He just said, "WOW, all this for me?" Excitedly, I smiled and said, "Yes baby, you deserve it!" I explained to him that I know we've been bumping heads lately and the last thing I want is for our marriage to be unsuccessful. I also explained to him that for the next 30 days, I would be doing some nice gestures, just to show my appreciation and love for him. I apologized for any hurt that I may have caused him and told him that I'd try to be the best wife that I could be. He wouldn't stop smiling. He pulled out my chair, like a gentleman, and sat across from me. I blessed our food and we dug in. After we ate dinner, I told him to take a shower while I cleaned the kitchen. He did as I told him. And I did as I said. Afterwards I sat on the edge of the bed in our bedroom, waiting patiently for him to come out of our personal bathroom.

He opened the door and my eyes smiled. He smelled so good. I knew he had on his Polo black cologne. His white polo towel was wrapped around his waist. I bit my bottom lip and he showed nothing but dimples. I locked the bedroom door and I walked up to him. I kissed his lips, took his towel off and dropped it to the floor. Our eye contact never faded. I got down on my knees and held his waist. I let my husband enter my mouth with his shaft. The only thing on my mind was to please him. I went in for the kill. I know my husband, so once I felt his body shaking; I knew it was a wrap. He grabbed my hair tight and bit his lip.

My mission was accomplished. His eyes said it all. He let go of my head and smiled. In a whispering voice I said. "Did you like it?" "I loved it", he said. He then lifted me off of the floor, and pulled me up to him, so that we're facing each other. He passionately kissed me and walked me over to the bed. He laid me down, turned off the light, and then crawled under the blanket. Let's just say we had a great night.... Day 1....

Day 2- Massage

Throughout my husband's work day, he often texts me to let me know how his day is going. Well, today he told me that he hurt his back while working on a machine. I knew he would want to come home and just relax. I had a great idea in mind! My timing is always perfect when it comes to him getting home. So once he walked through the door everything was intact. The house was clean, the girls were asleep, and his food was in the microwave.

After he heated up his food and ate, he got in the shower. That was my que to get ready really fast! I pulled out my bag of tea light candles and set them up all over our bedroom. The dresser and chest was covered with tea light candles. I placed the massage oil on the bed and I had it propped up on some pillows. I hurried and lit every candle. I was nervous that he would catch me in the act but he didn't. When I heard the shower turn off, I kicked the bag under the bed so he wouldn't see it. By the time he opened the bathroom door, all he could see is the reflection on the walls from the candle flames and my shadow on the wall. Tonight I decided to wear nothing but my red bra, red boy shorts and a red satin robe. It was perfect!

I smiled and said, "Welcome to my massage parlor! It's called "Tres' Joli'"... His smile was huge. He said "Very pretty is the name?" We both laughed and I smacked his arm. "Yes!" I said...You like? He said "I love it Jo". I had him lay on his stomach, to give him a body massage. I began at his feet. By the time I got to his thighs he was very relaxed. I worked my way up his back, over to his shoulders, then down his back again. I gave him a full body massage and he loved every minute of it. I told him to turn around. As soon as he laid on his back his soldier was at attention. I smiled and I immediately gave him a happy ending that he'd never forget. Day 2...

Day 3- Indoor Picnic

      11:08 pm and I heard the door unlocking. I hurried into my bathroom to spray on my "Secret Craving body mist" by Victoria's Secret and ran to the door. I looked through the peep hole and told my husband that he could NOT have his eyes open when entering our apartment. So it was no surprise to him when he saw me standing right by the door, with a scarf to cover his eyes. I guided him to the bedroom where he showered and changed out of his work clothes. I already had his towel and shorts next to the sink.

      I also had the living room set up. I had a huge black faux fur blanket on the floor. There were eight throw pillows around the blanket leaning on our sectional. They were black and brown. I had a cute nice sized wicker picnic basket on the middle of the blanket. I typically make a hot meal for my family, but this night I took another route. I made us some turkey sandwiches, with tomatoes, lettuce and cheese. I put some strawberries in a plastic container and I sprinkled a little sugar on them. I also put some grapes in a zip lock bag. I had a few bottled waters and some small bags of chips, just in case he wanted extra. My husband is not a big beer drinker so I put a few Smirnoff's in the basket as well. We were all set!

      Now I'm just waiting for him. Looking at my fresh mani and pedi, Dee broke my concentration yelling out like a child on punishment. "Can I come out now!!?" I smiled and ran out to the door of our bedroom. "Yes you can" I said, "But you have to keep your eyes closed!" I walked him into the living room and said "open your eyes". He smiled once he saw the little set up. He looked at the picnic basket in the middle of the floor. I said "We're having an indoor picnic!" He always gets a kick out of how excited I am about the smallest things. He smiled and gave me a hug and kissed my forehead. "Thanks sweetheart," he said to me. I pulled out all of the food and passed him his sandwich. I was really proud of myself. Something so small can mean so much to someone! I looked up to give him a bottled water and he was already watching me. I blushed a little... He gives me chills, and to see how he's really appreciating the things I've been doing for him, makes me want to do more... We enjoyed our food. We talked and laughed all night. No cell phones, no TV... Just us... Day 3...

Day 4- Movie Date and Drinks

"Good morning beautiful," my husband said. The sun from the window hit my face as Dee opened the blinds. My eyes were still closed but I smiled. Dee is by far a morning person, so when I heard those words, I knew he was in a good mood. He never talks like that! Just hearing that melted my heart. "Hey Poppa", I replied. I saw his dimples on the side of his face as he smiled. He loved when I called him Poppa. I asked him did he have any plans that day. He said that he only wanted to get a haircut. I thought to myself, "Perfect!" I told him that I would get dressed and ride with him, and after his hair cut, I was taking him on a date. We quickly got ready and we left. After Dee got his hair cut, he pulled out his wallet to pay his barber. I rushed over and gave him the 20 dollars to pay for it. He just smiled.

We left the barber shop and went straight to Solon Movie Theater. We love this theater! It's pretty quiet and they have a bar inside, as well as a game room. We walked in, I paid for our tickets and we headed straight to the concession stand. I had him pick out whatever he wanted to snack on. When I took my money out of my wallet to pay the cashier, I gave Dee a side grin. I said "I'm taking you places... meeting people". Then I gave the cashier my money. We all started laughing. He knew that was a phrase from one of our favorite movies, House Party. I'm such a movie-head! We had about twenty minutes before the movie started, so we walked over to the bar. Dee ordered himself a Long Island Iced Tea, and I ordered me a Strawberry Mango Martini. It totally gave me life! As we sat there, I let Dee know how much I love him and appreciate him, and enjoyed hanging out with him.

We ordered another drink and took them into the theater. We noticed that we were the only ones in there. That totally made me smile. I have to admit, my mind is in the gutter ninety percent of the time. Dee must've read my mind, because he instantly said "Dude don't even think about it". I just laughed and told him to chill out. I didn't do anything... (side smirk) Yet!

Anyways, we enjoyed our drink and movie... And a little bit of this and that...
Day 4...

Day 5- Sunday Football

Sundays... The day that the man watches football ALL DAY LONG!! And it's nothing wrong with that... I have to admit, Sunday football actually makes my 31 days a lot easier for me. I decided that on Sundays, I'd cater to all of Dee's needs. I'd make sure he had all of the "football snacks," that he wanted. I'd also make sure that the girls stayed out of his way and that only HE could keep the remote. That's major in our house! Humorous right?

Well, the day before, I went to the store and grabbed a few items. I bought some of his favorite snacks. This consists of Pork Rinds, Tostitos and Salsa, Kit Kats, plain chips and dip and a case of beer. When dee sat on the couch, I purposely walked passed him with a switch in my hips, to go into the kitchen. I loved knowing I could still catch my husband's eye. I bent over to get the beers out the fridge and before I could stand up all the way, I felt Dee pressed against me. I grinned and stood up.

He wrapped his arms around me, smelled my hair and kissed my neck. "Looking good in those shorts Mrs. Fort," he said hungrily as he squeezed my cheeks. I blushed and turned around with a huge smile on my face. "Thank you Mr. Fort", I replied. "Here"! I gave him his beers. He laughed and said "you bought beers Joli"? He knows that I NEVER buy beer. I still had a huge grin on my face and I proudly said, "YES"!! "Today I'm going to cater to your every want and need. I bought you more snacks, I'll bring them to you when you go sit down". That smile always does it for me! I could tell he was kind of shocked. "Wow, thank you" he said. Although Dee is not a huge beer drinker, he still enjoyed a nice cold brew from time to time.

I walked him back in to the living room and pushed him on the couch. "Now stay!!" We both started laughing and when I tried to walk away, he grabbed my hand and pulled me on to his lap. "You stay", he said, and he sat up. He laid me down and started kissing my neck. He went lower and lower and began kissing my stomach, to my thighs. He slowly moved the bottom of my shorts to the right and indiscreetly exposed me. He passionately kissed me and took me to ecstasy. Needless to say, he missed the first half of the football game.

Once we were done, I got up to get his snacks as I planned to do before he stopped me. As I grabbed his chips, I smiled and thought to myself, "I absolutely love this man!" I softly said, "Thank you Lord". Not more than one week ago, I thought my marriage was over, and within a few days, I see a difference. Out of my thoughts and prayer, I skipped like a kid into my living room and gave my husband his tray full of snacks. He kissed my lips and said, "Thanks again Jo". With a smirk on my face, I said "No, thank you... Supa head!!" We both laughed. "Ok, I got you", he said. I told him if he needed anything, I'd be in the room. "Enjoy you're your game Poppa"... Day 5...

Day 6- The Amazing Grapefruit

I can openly admit that I'm a very sexual woman. My husband knows this. I may try anything once. Twice, if I like it. Twelve times if I love it! No, seriously, I love spicing things up with my husband. So there was no doubt in my mind that I would be trying this grapefruit thing I heard about.

After Dee took his shower, I had a chair sitting right in front of the bathroom door. I was sitting, Indian style next to "THE CHAIR". "THE CHAIR" had black rose petals around it. He had no idea of what to expect. I wanted him to believe that anything could happen in this chair, and to sit at his own risk! "It's all in the presentation", I said with a devilish grin. He began smiling when he saw me. I smiled myself just looking at his body. Yikes! My husband is one attractive man. All types of sexiness beneath this towel. What stood out most was the print at the front of the towel... OUCH! I thought to myself, Thank you Lord!

He interrupted my thoughts and asked me why I was sitting on the floor. I didn't answer him. I just snatched off his towel and placed it on the chair and told him to have a seat. He did as I told him. He sat down completely naked. I blind folded him and explained to him that he could not touch me. No matter how I made him feel, again I stressed that he could NOT touch me! UNLESS, I tell him otherwise.

He agreed. I pulled a small plate from underneath our bed. I had the grapefruit on it. Not just any grapefruit. THEE grapefruit. It was nice and juicy and at room temperature. I had already prepared the grapefruit by cutting a hole through the middle of it. The hole was about the size of his penis. I kneeled before my husband. I began to rub his thighs to his groin area and down to his knees. I actually did that a few times. Just to relax him a little. He seemed pretty nervous not knowing what was going on. I admired his muscular legs. It was no challenge to get his penis to attention. I slowly took him into my mouth. I shortly noticed his hands and feet shaking uncontrollably. I also noticed that he almost touched my head but he must have remembered the "no touching rule," so he grabbed the side of the chair.

I grabbed the grapefruit and gently slid it over his penis. At first he had a confused look on his face. I admit I was kind of nervous because I didn't know how he would react. I knew what I was doing, so that didn't concern me so much. I began to stroke him with the grapefruit. It was nice and juicy. Once I saw him bite his lip, I thought to myself, Goteeeeeeem! I stroked him up and down in a circular motion using the grapefruit.

I started sucking him at the same time. Still stroking him with the grapefruit, I put my lips on the top of his penis and flicked my tongue back and forth. Nonstop. He grabbed the side of the chair and whispered "baby you're about to make me cum"... I didn't stop until he exploded in my mouth. I stood up, licked my lips and smiled. He leaned back on the chair and threw his head back. A huge smile appeared on his face. I let him know that he could not remove the blindfold as of yet. I walked to our bathroom and grabbed a warm towel to wipe him off. I sat the towel on the dresser and stood over my husband. I kissed his lips. "Are you ready for more", I asked?

He smiled and said "yes." I told him he's free to touch me now. He used his hands to explore my body. It was kind of funny to me. With his blind fold still on, he was excited like a kid in the candy store. He started to touch my waist then went lower to my butt, then my upper back, then my butt again. As if he was trying to figure out where he should start. I then took off his blind fold. When he saw me naked I knew that playtime was over. Our eyes locked. I'm sure you can figure out how our night ended... Day 6

Day 7- Coupon Booklet

For day 7, I kept it really simple. I decided to give my husband a coupon booklet. But not just any type of coupon booklet. A coupon booklet that he could actually use, at any time, no matter what the situation is, or how I felt. Many times in marriages/relationships, you may argue and you don't want to deal with each other at all. You might feel neglected because your partner is doing their own thing and you might just want some attention.

Well these coupons will definitely come in hand. Now, I specifically told Dee that he could not use these coupons while I'm doing my 31 days of pleasing him. They have to be used after the Month of October. Once he's able to use the coupons, I agreed that I MUST do whatever the coupon says no matter what time it is.

To make my booklet, I used a sheet of construction paper and I cut it into the size that I wanted my booklet to be. After I typed up the coupons, I taped them inside of the booklet and stapled it together. I even decorated it. Gave it a little love and BOOM! My coupon booklet was done. Here are a few ideas that I thought of, to write for the coupons. I chose things that I know he loves:

FULL BODY MASSAGE

ARGUMENT FREE PASS- No matter what I am upset about, I agree to no longer be upset, nor will I argue or bring up the argument again (I decided to give him two of these because I know I can be a handful at times)

MAKE YOU SOMETHING TO EAT, YOUR CHOICE, ANYTIME

HAIR CUT FEE

NICE HOT BUBBLE BATH

BOTTLE OF CIROC W/ A PEPSI

MEAL AT PIADA

ANY SEXUAL FAVOR AT ANYTIME

A DAY OF CATERING TO YOUR EVERY WANT AND NEED

GROCERY STORE RUN

Day 8- Love Note and Small Gift

Sometimes the simplest things can mean so much. Before Dee woke up, I placed a card on the table, next to his lunch bag. Inside the card I wrote a sweet note that read:

"Hi Poppa. I hope you have a wonderful day at work. This evening is all about you. Whatever you want me to do, I'll do it. Whatever you want to eat, I'll make it or buy it. I just want to show you how much I appreciate you. You are a brilliant man. I absolutely LOVE how you go to work every day and make sure the kids and I have what we need. I admire you and the love you have for us. Thank you. You are appreciated."

Love,

Your Sweetheart

Also, he loves pistachios, so I bought him a few small bags that he can snack on. My husband works in a Steel Mill. I often get text saying "I'm starving", "I wish I had something to snack on until my lunch." With that on my mind, I thought pistachios were the perfect snack for him. So I put the small packs in a heart shape, on the kitchen table. He smiled when he saw it. Seeing those dimples were validation that he loved it. He pulled me into him and gave me a kiss and a hug. He said, "I love you and appreciate you". I smiled and returned the kiss. "I love you too Dee," I said.

Needless to say, we had a great evening. Of course he wanted me to play the Xbox one with him and he wanted seafood for dinner. I prepared some crab legs, scampi's, asparagus and baked potatoes. He was very pleased. Day 8...

Day 9- Another Woman

I sat on the couch, very nervous. I'm not sure how Mr. Fort will react tonight, once he meets me. I'll soon find out though. By the way, my name is Sincere. Mr. Fort will be calling me by my nick name... Sin. I am a virgin, and I'm very shy. But tonight, I'm here to please Mr. Fort and cater to his every need. So I must throw that "virgin mentality" out the door. His wife instructed me to do so. I'm sure he'll admire my outfit that she picked out for me.

I must say, his wife has great taste. I ran to the full body mirror in their bedroom, just to make sure I looked ok. I wore a long fitted satin gown, with a white thong underneath. Wearing all white makes my cocoa brown skin complexion stand out. I really like it. I feel like a queen. Mrs. Fort instructed me to wear my long tresses straight, because that's what her husband likes.

Also, I had to have a fresh mani and pedi with French tips. I must say, I kind of feel like a slut, considering the fact that she paid for all of this. But, oh well, I'd do anything for her. She's such a great woman. She'd do mostly anything to please her husband. Interrupting my thoughts, I heard Mr. Fort's key in the door. I quickly ran into the living room and stood next to the couch.

Timidly, I looked to the ground when he entered, while twiddling my fingers. I glanced over to see that Mr. Fort was staring at me. He smiled. I immediately looked back to the ground. That man was gorgeous! I thought to myself. He has big dimples and pretty white teeth. I wasn't prepared for that. I even have a wet feeling in my panties. I'm scared! Oh no, here he comes, I thought to myself.

"What's up wit you?" he said. I blushed and gestured my hand to shake his. Still looking to the ground. "Hello Mr. Fort, my name is Sincere. You can call me Sin. Your wife hired me, to cater to all of your needs while she's away for the night," I said. "All of my needs?" he asked. "Yes sir," I said. "She gave me instructions as well. Your food is in the microwave, and I put your toiletries on the bathroom sink, for when you're done with your shower sir," I said. Nodding his head, "Ok, Sincere is it?" he asked. "Yes sir", I said.

"Did my wife instruct you to please me in the bedroom as well?" he asked. "Yes sir", I said. "Good, will you go fetch my food and heat it up so I can eat and take my shower?" he asked. Ok... I'm trying really hard to stay in character but my husband is not helping the situation by saying fetch. I'm laughing so hard on the inside. "Yes sir, Mr. Fort," I said, and I did as I was told.

After he ate his food, he told me to wait on the bed for him, once he got out the shower. I nodded my head and went into the bedroom. Dee walked out the bathroom completely naked. I had a nervous look on my face. "What's wrong Sincere?" Dee asked. "I'm a bit nervous Mr. Fort." I've never been with a man before", I said. His right eyebrow rose.

"So you've only effed with broad's hunh"? He said. Again... My husband is making it so hard for me to stay in character! But I stood my ground and didn't laugh! "No Mr. Fort, I've never had sex before," I said. Mr. Fort laughed and said to himself, "So my wife hired somebody who don't know how to suck my dick? Classic!" Although I wanted to laugh, I was still doing great by keeping a serious face. "Mr. Fort, I promise, I can please you just as well as your wife does," I said. "Sincere, sweetheart, I doubt that seriously, but it's a worth a try. Lay down on the bed," he said. I did as I was told. Dee sat in front of me on the bed and pushed my gown over my thighs exposing my panties. He then grabbed the top of my thighs and began to squeeze and rub them.

"Sincere your thighs are nice and thick, and your skin is so soft and smooth," he said. I began to blush. Mr. Fort's penis began to rise. I didn't know what that meant, so I closed my eyes. Still rubbing my thighs, Dee said, "Sincere I'm gonna give you head, do you know what that is?"

"No sir," I said. He pulled my panties off and threw them to the floor. "Well I'm going to show you what it is. Are you ready Sin," he asked me. I just nodded my head. He then licked my entire vagina. My back arched and I moaned. Mr. Fort then began to suck my clitoris. I thought I was about to pee on myself but it was different. My legs started to shake and I could barely breathe. "Mr. Fort!" I screamed. I pushed his head up, to stop him from sucking me.

He stopped and licked his lips and smiled at me. Breathing heavily I sat up. "It's your turn to do that to me Sincere, can you handle that?" he asked. "I can try sir," I said. "Now Sincere, my wife is really good at this, don't disappoint me," he said. Again I nodded my head to confirm that I understood him. I slowly begin to lick his penis. "BOOOOOOO, this corny!" Dee said, and he started laughing. "Mr. Fort, it would help if you didn't do that," I said. "Well Sincere, you need to handle your business better. Don't nobody want a wack dick sucker. Get that shit together. Think of it as your trying to suck the juice out of a Popsicle. You go up and down and use your tongue. You might gag a little, but that means nothing, you're just doing it right," he said, and then smiled at me.

"Yes sir," I said. I then put my mouth over his entire penis. I sucked and licked until Mr. Fort was pulling my hair. I spit on his penis and used my hand to stroke him. I continued to lick and suck him until he exploded in my mouth. He looked like he was having a seizure, but it was kind of funny. Now I'm smiling at him. "Did I do it right Mr. Fort?" I asked. He just smiled and nodded his head yes. He then patted my head and said "That was actually better than my wife Sincere." I just smiled. Mr. Fort quickly turned me around and thrust his penis inside of me.

He was so rough, but I loved it! He continued to go in and out of me, grabbing my hair and smacking my butt. I was moaning and screaming and Mr. Fort let out a roaring sound and yelled out" Sin!" We collapsed on the bed at the same time. Both of us were breathing heavily. I turned around and started to stare at him.

He was so attractive. I see why his wife loves him so much. "I love you Mr. Fort," I said. He opened his eyes and said, "Don't start that shit bitch, you need to leave before my wife comes home, and lock the door behind you." We both busted out laughing. He kissed my lips. "You crazy man," he said. I smiled. "Did you like it?" I asked.

"It was cool, but dude, I felt like I was really fucking another bitch! Don't do that shit no more!" We both laughed and cuddled. "I love you Poppa," I said. He kissed my forehead. "I love you too Mrs. Fort," he said. "Oh and I ain't forget!" I said. I punched him in his stomach. "It was better than your wife nigga?" We laughed again and he kissed me. "You know you the best sweetheart", he said. I just smiled and we then went to sleep. Day 9...

Day 10- Movie Night

Friday night!! I absolutely love Friday nights! Since my husband and I are off on Saturdays, I figured we could have a movie night. The girls are staying at my moms, so it would be some nice alone time. I decided to find something on Netflix. Yeeeah... We'll Netflix and Chill tonight. That was a little dry humor for you.

Anyway, I went to the store to get some of our favorite snacks. To name a few, I grabbed some Werther's caramel popcorn, milk duds, sour patch kids, nachos with cheese and salsa, and a few pops. A bunch of junk food. Some may not want to go the "junk food route" and get some healthy snacks... Totally fine! However, I myself prefer to be on some trash tonight...

When Dee walked in, he looked at me and instantly smiled. I was sitting down Indian style with a messy bun and a huge smile on my face. Looking like an anxious kid. I wore my Victoria's Secret onesie. You know I had to keep it cute. After we greeted each other with a kiss, I took his work bag and sat it on the kitchen table. I helped him remove his jacket and I hung it on the chair. Dee walked up behind me and wrapped his arms around my waist and kissed my face again. As he walked over to the microwave to see if his food was in there, he asked, "What's up for tonight?"

We're having a movie night tonight, so babe, please don't be screaming like you did the last time we watched a horror movie," I said. I attempted to keep a serious face when I said that, but when I saw him looking at me with a straight face, I busted out laughing. "Ha ha ha" he said, with no smile. I suddenly saw his dimples showing. I knew he thought it was funny. "Move night? That's cool, let me jump in the shower so we can get our night started," he said. We had a very peaceful night. We watched our movies, and enjoyed each other's time. Day 10...

"Father God, I come to you today because I'm tired Lord. I'm asking you to give me strength. Please help me to not feel overwhelmed as I continue to do my 31 days. Please give me energy to please my husband and to continue to show him love. Lord I love you and I thank you for everything you've done for me Lord, In Jesus name, Amen" - Joli Michelle

Day 11- Gas Her Up

Today we're going to Columbus to go to my son's track meet. Normally when we leave for Columbus, my husband stops at the gas station to get him something to drink, and he fills up the gas tank. Maybe even an energy drink. Well, because I knew we were going, the day before I did a little shopping of my own.

I bought all of his normal snacks and drinks. I even filled up the gas tank so he didn't have to stop at all. I cooked us a big breakfast so that we wouldn't have to stop at a restaurant. You know, save a few bucks. I even packed us some sandwiches and fruit, just in case we got hungry.

The backseat was covered with colorful gift bags that I bought from the dollar store. Even the water had its own gift bag. Yeah, I admit, I was being a little extra with it. I figured I'd make a simple surprise look bigger than what it actually was. When Dee got in the car I was already smiling. Of course he smiled at me, he said "What's up, why you so happy"? He never knew what I had planned.

I said "TADAAAAAAAAH!!!" Pointing my arms and hands to the backseat. He turned around and saw all of the gift bags. He laughed. My husband knows that I'm a kid at heart so everything excites me! Especially when I'm doing something for someone else. He started looking in all the bags. "What's all this?" he asked.

I told him that for Day 11 of pleasing him, I wanted to take care of everything for our road trip. I filled up the gas tank, bought all of the snacks as well. I wanted to make sure he didn't have to spend a dollar.

Also, I put twenty dollars in an envelope that read "For my Poppa." Just in case I didn't grab something that he wanted. "Wow, thank you," he said. He then grabbed my chin and kissed my lips. "You're the best sweetheart, that's what's up".

In my language, that meant, "YOU'RE THE BEST WIFE EVER BABY, I LOVE YOU!!!!" His kisses always made me blush. We then buckled up and was ready to roll... My Day 11...

Day 12- Luxurious Bubble Bath

We all know my usual Sunday Football routines. Not today. Although I made sure Dee had everything he wanted to watch his football games, I thought I'd get him relaxed for the night. Football was finally over. My husband was so into the game that he didn't notice anything I did around the house. He stood up and stretched. When he turned around I had his plate on the dining room table with a nice glass of wine. He walked over to the table and sat down and started to eat.

"Un Un, you better bless your food homie!" I said to him. He chuckled, "my bad" he said. He bowed his head and prayed to himself and started to eat. "You like?" I asked. He turned around with a mouth full of food and gave me thumbs up, but then his facial expression changed.

Which it should have! I was standing behind him naked. Well not completely naked. I wore an apron that read, "World's Greatest Wife" on the front of it. It covered the front of my body and tied in the back. I had on my sexy black pumps and I did a twirl. I put my hands on my knees and started doing a mini twerk, singing "butt naked nasty or naw aaaaye." He covered his mouth as if he was about to spit out his food from laughing. We both started laughing. That's one thing I love about us. I can be myself. Sexy or silly, he never judges me. He'll just join right in.

After he swallowed his food he just laughed and said, "you stupid man, come here." That flirty smile on his face and little head nod let me know what time it was. I walked over to him but instead of sitting on his lap, I pulled him up.

"I have a surprise for you," I said. "Is it a grape fruit?" he asked. We both laughed. "No crazy! Come here and I'll show you," I said. He rushed to finish his food, grabbed his glass of wine and started to walk with me. I took his hand and while we walked through the kitchen, I could see that he noticed the trail of red rose petals. We walked down the hall and the trail continued all the way to the bathroom.

Anxiously I said, "Go ahead, open the door!" with a huge smile on my face. He opened the door and the lights were out. The bathroom was lit with tea light candles and two Mango scented candles from Bath and Body Works. I love that scent!

Rose petals were spread across the floor, going directly to the tub. There were candles along the side of the tub, as well as the sink. Steam arose from the bubble bath. He was speechless. He could only smile. I said, "Babe you're such a hard worker, I just want you to relax tonight. Take off your clothes and get in the tub, if you need anything just call me."

My husband is on his feet all day, and he really is a hard worker, so he deserves this. I know he had a long week ahead of him and it's my job to make sure that when he's home, that everything is good. "Thanks Jo," he said, and kissed my cheek. Once he got in the tub, I washed his back for him and I left out so that he could relax and enjoy his bath. Day 12...

Day 13- Insurance Lady Prank-

The Text messages

10:15 p.m. Me: Babe... Did you really have an insurance agent come over this late, and not tell me? There's a woman here saying that you told her that you weren't available during the day and to come when you got off of work.

10:17 pm. Dee: That broad is a damn lie! I'd never make an appointment this late at night! Where is she from? She's at our house right now?

10:18 pm. Me: Yeah she's here. She's from Progressive. Don't we have State Farm?

10:18 pm. Dee: Joli look at how late it is! Why would you even let her in! smh I'll be there in a minute. That broad aint gon be happy with this conversation.

11:00 pm

      I heard Dee's key in the lock. He walked in with an evil look on his face. When he saw me, his whole facial expression changed. To give you a brief description of what he saw... I was sitting on the couch with my legs crossed. I had on a hot pink laced thong with the matching bra. It was only right to have my cheeks out. I had on some black BCBG gladiator heels, and a white apron that says Progressive on the front of it. The apron only covered the front of my body, but the back was out like PLADOW!!! I wore my hair in a curly bun. I wanted to accessorize a tiny bit so I wore my diamond studs and my BCBG reading glasses.

      When Dee looked at me, it was like a breath of fresh air for him. His smile was as if he was at peace. I walked over to him reaching my hand out to shake his. "Hi Mr. Fort, my name is Jo, I'm with Progressive Insurance. Your wife felt as though you needed to upgrade your policy so I'm here to assist you with that." Dee laughed and said, "Dude that

Insurance broad was about to get cussed out!" I interrupted him by saying, "Sir, I don't know what you're speaking of, but I'd like to keep this professional." He just smiled and nodded his head.

I grabbed his lunch bag and pulled him by his hand and led him to the sofa. "Also Mr. Fort, your wife is gone for the night and she asked me to explain everything to you. Before she left she carefully read over all of the documents and signed them. I need you to look over the policy as well sir and sign here." I pointed to the X with my fresh manicured nails and passed him the pen. Although my husband doesn't say it much, I know he admires how I keep myself up. I'm a very simple person, not flashy at all. But I'm still a woman and love to be pampered. I could rock some Tim's and a sweat suit and still be sexy. He loves that about me. But to see this outfit on me, I noticed that he couldn't keep his eyes off of me.

Of course I made up the policy myself. I basically typed up a policy with a few prices. The policy consisted of things that I thought my husband would enjoy. I put demonstration next to the different policies, so that Mr. Fort could get a sense of what he was paying for. For example...I typed:

LIPS (demonstration)

ASS (demonstration)

TONGUE (demonstration)

Signature was on the bottom of the page. Just to give you a brief description of our policy. Since Mr. Fort was perplexed on what his policies entailed, I had to give him a few demonstrations. I showed him what benefits came with LIPS package. He was very pleased to see how satisfying that package was. It targeted the neck, the mouth, the stomach, even below the belt! I personally think that's a great package. He seemed really interested to see the ASS demonstration. I basically showed him how it moves, at every angle. Once I showed him what's done with the TONGUE demonstration it was a wrap! Needless to say, the documents were signed, and Mr. Fort purchased all three of my policies. Day 13...

Day 14- Sextivities

Sextivities will be a night full of wonderful sexual activities!! Hopefully you saw the excitement in my words. I went to Ambiance and bought some games that I felt would interest my husband. No one knows your mate like you do. So to pick out some fun games should be a piece of cake. Once Dee came home he took his usual shower and ate his food.

Once he walked out of our personal bathroom, he caught me lying on my stomach, shuffling some cards that read SEX on them. He smacked my behind and kissed my forehead. I looked over and saw his dimples. I began to smile and I said "ugh thirsty, what you smiling for!" All I could see was his teeth. The fulfillment of anticipation in his eyes was awesome! Excitedly he said "Nothing! I'm just curious to know what you have planned for tonight!" Just seeing his reactions these last few days, I'm not shocked that he comes home looking forward to something new. If someone planned to do something special for me for 31 days straight, I'd probably call off of work!

Anyways, Instead of keeping him waiting, I explained to him all of the activities that I had planned for us, for the night. I had a board game called Let's F*&%... Yeah... pretty explicit game. I loved it! I also had a card game that read SEX. Last but not least, I had some sex dice. They had images of different sexual positions on each block. He seemed to be very pleased with the games and my plans. He sat next to me on the bed and said "Let the games begin!"... Day 14...

Day 15- Video Game Night

For Day 15, I decided to do a video game night because my husband loves to play video games! On the other hand, I can most definitely go without them. BUT since he likes it, I'll love it... for a night, that is! When Dee came home from work, he was shocked to see that I had controllers set out and the Call of Duty game on the big screen. I wore some cute gray jogging pants and one of his t shirts. I had my hair up in a bun and I was ready for war!

As always he smiled when he saw me. I said "Yo, you ready to get whooped on Son!" (In my most creative New York accent) He could only laugh at me. I told him to hurry up and shower as I prepared everything. I heard the oven timer go off. I jumped up to get the hot wings out of the oven. I had already cut up the celery, and put the ranch dressing in a small glass bowl. I grabbed our glasses with ice, and pulled his favorite pop out the freezer. It was nice and cold.

By the time he got out of the shower, I had all the food in the living room and I was ready to play. Once Dee came in and sat down, like always, I let him know how much I love him. I told him that I decided to do a video game night because I know he hasn't been able to play as much as he'd like too, since I've tied up his evenings. I could see that he was happy with this. I grabbed my controller and said sooo... let's do it! How do I play? We both laughed and he told me what to do. We had a really good time... Day 15

"Dear Heavenly father, I come to you today because Lord I need you. Things are going great with my husband. But Lord, a part of me is hurt. I keep thinking to myself, why doesn't he do this for me? Why am I the one catering to his needs, when I wasn't feeling loved? All I ever wanted was for him to show me love father. I don't understand. I just want him to compliment me and show me that he cares. I want my husband to show that he appreciates what I do, Lord. Please get rid of these ill feelings that I'm having. Please help me to keep a positive attitude and please guide me in the right direction. I love you and I thank you in advance Lord. In Jesus name, Amen"

-Joli Michelle

Day 16- Positive Sticky Notes

I'm halfway through my 31 days!! I'm so excited to share what I did for my husband with all of you! It can be so overwhelming to think of different things to do, EVERY SINGLE DAY, FOR A MONTH, for one person! With that being said, sometimes you just don't have the extra money to do certain things. So for day 16, I kept it really simple and I wrote positive notes to my husband.

I bought a pack of sticky notes. On each sticky, I wrote positive things, that I felt fit my husband. *"I love your dimples"*, *"Your smile is everything to me"*, *"I love the way you feel inside of me"*, *"You're so smart"*, *"I admire your ambition"*.....Those are just a few examples of what I wrote.

I stuck the notes all over our bathroom mirror and on the mirror above our dresser. He couldn't even see himself because I covered every inch. Needless to say, he was happy. And that was my Day 16...

Day 17- Movie of His Choice

For Day 17, I decided to have Dee pick a movie for us to watch, as well as his choice of dinner for the night. He decided on "Dawn of the Dead" and for dinner, he wanted to eat Tilapia, broccoli and cheese, white buttered rice and some rolls. Easy...

I let him know what my plans were before he left out for work this morning. That way, I could have everything prepared before he arrived home. Today is one of those days where I really just wanted to come home and relax. But of course, I had to make sure my family was taken care of before that could happen.

Cooking dinner and letting him choose a movie was perfect timing for me. I have to admit, my days of pleasing him, are becoming overwhelming. I'm pushing through though. Our evening ended up being nice and chill. It was a great way to end our work week... Day 17...

Day 18- SWEETEST DAY Surprises!

      I can't speak for everyone, but I LOVE holidays! May it be, Martin Luther King Day, Veterans Day, Labor Day, July 4th, Christmas or Valentine's Day. You name it, I love it! Especially if I'm off of work!! For this Sweetest Day, I wanted to do something that I'd never done before. I've surprised my husband many times, but never like this! A few days ago, I called and made an appointment with his barber. I made sure his slot would not be taken and I paid him in advance. Now I can start our day!

      My husband loves Bob Evans, so I decided to take him there for breakfast. We walked in and the greeter showed us to our table. When Dee went to sit down, I hurried and gave our waitress a gift box. I explained to her what I was doing and that I wanted her to bring the gift to our table, with my husband's food. After a few minutes she came and took our order. I grabbed his hands and said to him, "See, I'm taking you places, meeting people," I promise that quote will never get old to us! We both started laughing. The waitress broke up our laughter when she arrived with our food.

      Dee noticed the navy blue box with silver stripes on it. You already know I was smiling with excitement! He looked at me. I said, "Open it! I'm having a panic attack here!" He opened the box and inside it was a new wedding ring. He looked really surprised. He looked at me again with a serious face. "Wow sweetheart, thank you," he said. Just to get you guys caught up on the wedding ring situation; A few years ago, Dee's wedding ring was split in half at his job. He would still wear the ring, but it would pinch his finger. It got to the point where he could no longer wear it. I told myself many times, that as soon as I could afford it, I'd buy him a new ring. So today was the day I gave it to him. He put the ring on and kissed me.

"Thanks again sweetheart," he said. I couldn't stop smiling. I think I was happier than he was! After the gift and kisses, we ate our food and left.

Next, I drove us to his hair cut appointment. We walked in and right away, his barber sat him down. He put the cape around Dee and said, "Oh yeah, here you go my man, your secret admirer told me to give this to you." Dee looked at me and of course, I could not hide my big smile! He opened up the box and inside was a black Movado watch. "You like it?" I asked full of excitement. "Yes I do," he said. All I saw was his dimples. I knew he didn't want to blush in front of the boys, but I knew he was happy. He got out of the barber's chair, hugged and kissed me and said thanks babe. I can see he was happy. That's all that mattered to me.

Once we left the barbershop, we went to a shopping center called Legacy Village. Dee and I loved to walk around there. We stopped at a chocolate shop called Rocky Mountain. They have the best chocolate covered strawberries that I've ever had! We walked in and the cashier said "Hello Mr. Fort, here are your items." Dee looked at me and smiled. He had no idea that I previously went in there and purchased him some goodies. I secretly winked at the cashier and whispered thank you to her. She smiled and gave me the thumbs up. We continued to walk around and did a little shopping.

Over all Dee had a really good day. Once we arrived home I walked into our dining room, and there were roses on the dining room table with my favorite chocolate candy. (turtles) There was an Edible arrangement on the table as well with a really sweet card. I was so caught up planning for Dee, I didn't think about him getting me anything! "Thanks Poppa!" I said. I ran and jumped on him and hugged him really tight. "You didn't think you were the only one with surprises did you?" he asked. I just gave him a kiss and smiled... Day 18

Day 19- A Time To Remember

Our wedding date is May 19th. So for Day 19, I decided to relive some of our fun times. What better way to do that, than pictures from our honeymoon at the Poconos. I wanted to show more of my creative side this time. It's a Sunday morning. I knew Dee would be sleeping in, so I knew I had some time to spare.

I quickly showered and got dressed. I rushed to the party store and bought 19 balloons with helium and strings attached. I also bought some tape. I chose white because I felt like it represented our wedding day. I returned home and Dee was still asleep. Perfect! I picked out 19 of my favorite honey moon photos. Some photos captured us at restaurants, some photos we were in a heart shaped Jacuzzi, some photos were of us at a comedy show, and some photos were of that handsome husband of mine. But overall, there were 19 pictures.

When Dee woke up, he opened his eyes to pictures in his face. It was hilarious! He sat up and smiled. "Joli, what is this?" He asked, as he began to pick and choose different balloons. I taped a different picture to the bottom of each balloon string. I told him that I thought I'd bring back some good memories. He started to laugh as he looked at some photos. I can tell it brought back many memories. He looked at every picture and spoke of some story to go with it. It was really nice seeing him so happy and starting his day off in a great mood. After he finished looking at the pictures, he said, "I really do love you Joli". He then gave me a hug. That hug showed me so much appreciation. And that was my day 19...

Day 20- Spicing It Up

I've said it before and I'll say it again. The 31days of pleasing my husband is just me showing my husband love and appreciation. I can do whatever I'd like. It's just a MUST that I do something for him, every day. For day 20, I was feeling myself. So every hour on the hour, I sent Dee a naked picture or a sexual video of me. I wanted him to be excited to see me later! Well it worked.

Once he arrived home, he wouldn't keep his hands off of me. He didn't even notice the card I bought, with one of his favorite snacks on top of it. I said, "Slow down Tiger! I bought you a card!" "Dude, you sent me pictures all day, I don't wanna see that right now, I'm trying to see what's under all this," he said while attempting to take off my pants. We both laughed. I admit, I was teasing him. BUT, I really wanted him to see my note. So I made him take the card anyway. Inside of the card I wrote a poem. It read:

Roses are blue, Violets are red, take off your clothes and get butt naked in this bed ☺ lol seriously... Hi Poppa! I know I say this to you a lot, but I want you to know that I admire the man that you are. I love you and I appreciate you. I know you have homework tonight, so I got you a small snack for you to enjoy. I love you...

And that was it! You don't always have to do anything major or spend money. Just like us women like to feel appreciated or even thought of, some of our fellas feel the same way. After he read the card, he kissed me and immediately took me in the bedroom. You know what happened next. Day 20...

Day 21- Foot Soak and Foot Rub

I know that I've mentioned over and over that my husband is a hard worker. He's also standing on his feet all day. Because he's not the type of man to just go and get a pedicure, I decided to give him a nice little foot soak. I had his dinner cooked by the time he came home. I could see in his eyes that he didn't know what I had in store for him that night. Seeing how anxious he's been to see what's next, is really keeping me motivated. I took a major risk this night. The girls were asleep when he arrived home. So... Why not give him a foot rub while being naked?

As always I could hear my husband's keys in the door. I held my breasts and ran over by the couch. Ladies you know we can't be running around with no bra on and breast flying everywhere. It hurts! I stood next to the couch with my hip poked out, attempting to look sexy. We both began laughing as soon as we made eye contact. I admit, I'm so silly that it's hard for me to keep a serious face. "Looking Good, Mrs. Fort," he said and he smacked my butt. I took his work bag and sat it down. I knew I'd hear his mouth about him being dirty and wanting to take a shower, so I had the towel in the bathroom already. He took a quick shower and threw on his basketball shorts.

I sat Dee down on the couch and put his feet in the hot bubbly water. I gave him his dinner and the remote control. I put some of my body oil in his water, to make his feet feel soft and smooth. I didn't say one word. He turned to Espn and relaxed. I gently rubbed and massaged his feet. Once I was done, I looked up and he was just smiling. His joy brings me joy. I smiled, got up and I emptied out the water. I rinsed his plate and put it in the kitchen sink. When I turned around my husband was standing in front of me. Again he smiled and said "thank you." He kissed my forehead and pushed me in front of him to walk into our bedroom. I knew he was staring at my body. So as I walked, I put a switch in every step! I had a huge grin on my face because the whole time, I was thinking to myself, "Yes hunty! Stare!" Dee closed the door behind us. We had an amazing night. Day 21...

Day 22- Wedding Reminder

Pictures are worth 1,000 words. For Day 22, I pulled out our wedding photos. Since the photos are put up, we never really sit down and look at them. Sooo... While Dee was at work, I gathered all of the wedding pics. I especially loved the "off guard" photos. In our bedroom, we have a bathroom with a glass shower.

Since I knew my husband would come straight home and get in the shower, I taped my favorite 22 pictures to the outside of the glass. That way when he showered he can look at all of the pictures. I knew they would put a smile on his face. Might be pretty corny to some, But it worked! He was very pleased with seeing all of our memories.

The joy in his eyes definitely showed when he saw the picture of his mom. She passed away a few years ago, so to see her picture meant a lot to him. Once he was done with his shower, he removed the pictures and we laid on the bed just laughing and reminiscing. We had a nice chill night. As long as he was smiling I knew I did well. Day 22...

Day 23- Desserts and Wine

      As soon as I started to prepare my chocolate covered strawberries, I knew that tonight's shenanigans would have us calling off of work the next day. I cut up some pineapples and I had some chocolate turtles as well. I was in such a sexual mood, that I honestly didn't care about dinner. As soon as my husband entered our apartment I knew I wanted to feel him inside of me. I couldn't wait to taste him. I knew he felt the same way when he saw me.

      I wore my red Victoria's Secret lace bra with the red thong to match, with a red lace garter belt attached. I left a little suspicion by covering up with my black satin robe. My hair was beautifully curled to the side, and I wore my black pumps. My diamond studs made my outfit complete. I felt as though he could see how bad I wanted him, when I bit my lip. I wanted to say "Ooh me so horny," But I knew I didn't want to bring any humor to this moment, and I knew we'd start laughing... I had to keep myself together tonight. I told myself. "Keep it sexy Joliiiii, keep it sexy!"

      He walked up to me and gave me a hug and a kiss and complimented my smell. "Thank you Mr. Fort," I said, and I took his hand and led him to the kitchen. I explained to him that tonight's menu was desserts and wine. He said "Jo that's cool, but what's up with dinner, I'm hungry as shit". I gave him the side eye. He knows what I'm in the mood for. Like seriously, who wants food at a time like this? Ok, I'm joking... But seriously! I'm trying to skip all of this. Besides... I already ate. I had to laugh myself at that thought.

      Since I know my husband so well, I already had his food in the microwave. After he finished his dinner I grabbed his hand and walked him to the bedroom. I had the wine and desserts set up on a pretty glass tray. The strawberries and pineapples were on separate plates, and I placed the grapes in a nice glass bowl. The turtles were also in a separate glass bowl. I placed a few rose petals on the bed, just to make it look sexy. I slowly fed him some strawberries and pineapples. I practically threw his wine down his throat. I wasn't playing games with him tonight!

He stood up and took off his shirt. I'm purposely lying on my stomach so he could get a peek of what was under the robe. I watched him through the mirror on our dresser. Oh he was looking alright! I know he liked what he saw because his manhood was growing and growing and growing through his boxers. My husband walked over to me and started kissing my neck. That was all she wrote!

The touch of his lips made my body quiver. After he teased me with his lips he flipped me over and went below my navel. He had me feeling like I was on an all-time high. He held the outside of my thighs until I stopped shaking. I laid there lifeless as he smiled. I couldn't move if I wanted too. He smacked my butt and said "Good night Mrs. Fort," and smiled. Who knew the tables would turn? A great night for me it was. Day 23...

Day 24- Free style Friday!!

       FREE STYLE FRIDAYS!!! The great thing about free style Friday is that you can do whatever you want! After my husband's shower last night we definitely decided to call off of work. (smile) First thing in the morning I dropped off our daughters at school. When I arrived home, surprisingly Dee was already out the shower and getting dressed. I had to catch up, real quick. I jumped in the shower, put on my lotion and got dressed.

       My husband wanted to get some breakfast so we decided to go to Bob Evans. His choice. We then went to Target to grab a few house cleaning products, and personal items. Then we decided to catch a matinee. I was so pumped! I loved going to the movies. Dee laughed at how excited I was. I let him choose the movie. It is about pleasing him, so why not? I bought us some snacks from the concession stand and we were set. Surprisingly, no one else was in the theater. That is absolutely PERFECT for someone as sexual as I am. I'm sure you're reading this like, she is a perv. But hey... It's my husband, don't judge me!

       We sat down and as fast as the previews were on the movie screen, I lifted up his shirt and unbuttoned his pants. He immediately knew, IT WAS ABOUT TO GO DOOOOWN!! I threw my jacket over my head. Just in case we had visitors. I slowly unzipped his pants and put his shaft into my mouth and pleased him. His body started shaking. Once his body was still and relaxed, I knew my mission was accomplished.

       I zipped up his pants and made him button them. He had a smile on his face. I wiped my mouth and said "So what did I miss?" "You mean what did WE miss!" he said. We both laughed. We kicked our feet up, he put his arm around me and he kissed my forehead. "I love you Mrs. Fort," he said. I said "I'd love me too". We laughed and just enjoyed the movie.

Once the movie ended, my husband wanted to stop and get some ink for our printer. I told him, "Whatever you wanna do poppa, we can do it." He's such a funny person, I knew there would never be a dull moment while we were out. We ran his errands and made it home before the girls did. For dinner he requested Tilapia, steamed veggies and a baked potato. I prepared dinner and we chilled for the rest of the night. Day 24...

Day 25- The Jet Hanger

This cold Saturday, I decided to take my husband to the Jet Hanger. It's an indoor sports facility. Typically when we go there, it's with the whole family. Well, I reserved the basketball court for a few hours to let Dee know that his wife GETS IT IN!!! Really I don't, BUT I play a good game. I told him to get dressed to play ball. Although his eye brow rose with concern, he didn't ask any questions. When he walked past me I saw his dimples. I know he was smiling and thinking, "I *got me a pretty dope wife*"... At least in my mind that's what he was thinking.

I quickly cooked us some pancakes and bacon, and poured a glass of orange juice. Quick and easy meal. We arrived at the Jet Hanger at 11 am on the dot. I couldn't wait for him to see my outfit!! I thought I was thee COLDEST WOMAN BALL PLAYER IN THE WORLD!! Blue is our favorite color, so I wore some black mid length Nike leggings with some short blue Nike shorts and a tank top to match it. I purposely made sure they were nice and short so I could distract him and dunk on him. Again, that's what I was going to do in my mind.

We're on the court. Eye to Eye. I'm dribbling the ball, acting as though I'm my favorite basketball player, Kobe Bryant. I said, "I'm about to murder you on this field son!" He shook his head and said "Court Joli...It's a Court." We laughed. I knew it was a court. I just wanted him to think I didn't know what I was doing.

I put up my index finger and said "ONE!" I threw the ball between his legs, grabbed his penis, and went for the hole. Boom! I gave him the business. "Dude are you serious? You can't do that, that's a foul!" he said. That's when I knew my husband couldn't see me on the court. I mean I always knew in my mind, that I had handles... But just now... I proved it. The score ended 20 to 2. Although I only had 2 points, it was a very productive day. I don't think I ever felt my husband up that many times in a day. I think we should play basketball more often. Day 25

Day 26- Clean out his car

  As a woman, a mother, a wife, a girlfriend... We have many roles! There may be times that we don't want to have sex! We don't want to clean, we don't want to cook, we literally don't want to do anything!! We might just feel tired and overwhelmed. We're house teachers, we're guidance counselors, we're chefs, we're maids, and the list goes on.

  Again, we have so many roles in our lives and homes that we just want to chill and do nothing! Well today was one of those days. I'm aggravated, annoyed, no energy. And I have cramps. Yes... This is that week. However, I told myself that no matter how I felt, for 31 days straight, I was doing some type of nice gesture for my husband. Today, I decided to clean out his car. That's something that my husband NEVER DOES! So I knew he would appreciate it.

  So as simple as it sounds, is as simple as it was. I took my husband's car to the drive thru car wash and had it washed. I then pulled around to the Air Vac, and I cleaned out his car. I even bought him a little air freshener and hung it on his mirror.

  Once I brought his car home, I parked it in his parking space and walked in the apartment. I didn't even tell him I was cleaning it out. Once he left to make a store run I knew he'd see it then, which he did. He walked in from the store and smiled and said "thank you," and kissed my cheek. It's the simple things that count. Day 26

DAY 27- Asian Food Night

Today was another "one of those days," but I'm going to be as positive as I can be. I'm sitting at my desk and I look at the clock. Thirty minutes left in the work day. I grabbed the phone and I called one of my favorite restaurants to order some carry out. I ordered two Hibachi Steak, Shrimp and scallop dinners, with fried rice and no onions, an order of two Volcano Rolls, California rolls and two Angry Dragon rolls. The girls requested pizza tonight so I placed an order for them as well.

Once I got home I started prepping for the night... I jumped in the shower, put on my lotion and threw on my Victoria secrets one piece thermal romper. Pulled my hair up in a cute bun and I was ready to decorate. I made a pallet on the floor, surrounded it with red and orange throw pillows. I placed two trays on the blanket. I kept our food in the oven until my husband got out of the shower. I got the girls together in there room, so they wouldn't have to come in the living room. I gave them their pizzas and drinks as well.

Dee arrived home ready to eat. I grabbed our food, made our plates and grabbed the chopsticks. My husband was always happy with my "presentations." He wasn't the type to just say it all the time, but I know he did. He would smile and nod his head. This time he actually said "Nice Job Mrs. Fort." That was enough for me. We had great conversation. No television or cell phones, just us, and we enjoyed each other's company and our meal. Day 27

Day 28- Game Stop

  Although dedicating 31 days to my husband is major, I have to admit, I feel a little selfish. I feel like I disregarded the things that he likes to do on a regular basis. I know he doesn't want to spend every single evening with me. Don't get me wrong, I don't mean that in a bad way.

  I just know my husband likes to play his X box one. He may want to hang with his brothers or anything. So today I didn't make plans. When I got off of work, I went to Game Stop and bought my husband a $50 gift card. I stopped at the store and bought a blank card.

  Inside of the card I wrote, "*I love you Poppa, enjoy.*" I put the gift card inside of the card and sealed the envelope. I came home and handed him the card, kissed his lips and started dinner. He seemed happy with the card, but then, he said "Sooo... What's up for the night?" I was in awe for a second. "What do you mean?" I asked. He said "Dude what's up, what did you plan for tonight?"

  I laughed because I didn't know he was actually looking forward to me doing things! I explained to him that I didn't want to be selfish and take up his evenings, so my gesture was the card. He said, "I love the card and the gift card Joli, BUT, don't ever think you're taking up my time. I've been looking forward to what you have in store for me when I get home."

  A huge smile came across my face. I jumped on him and said "Aww babe! Ok let's play Uno and Tunk!!" He smirked and said "Alright... BUT let's go to game stop first so I can buy me a new game daaawg!!" I was totally fine with that. Funny thing is that I felt kind of sad knowing that I was giving him his evening to himself.

Turns out we both felt the same way. We had a great evening. I made us some buffalo chicken salads, we played Uno and Tunk. I even played the X BOX game with him. And that was Day 28...

Day 29- Ice cream Run

      Lately I've been trying to eat healthier. So I don't buy a lot of snacks and junk food. The one thing Dee and I have a love for is ice cream. So for Day 29, I took him on an ice cream date! We went to one of our favorite spots, Baskin Robbins.

      We ordered two banana splits with butter pecan ice cream, hot fudge, nuts and whipped cream. He got his with cherries, I'm fine without them. I paid for our ice cream and we sat down. Mmmmm... It was everything my heart and soul desired! We talked, we laughed, and we ate our ice cream and came home.

      We were like teenagers going on a cheap date. As he talks, I just listen. I'm so in love with this man. It's my pleasure to do this for him. Day 29...

Day 30- Balloons of Appreciation

Ok so tomorrow is a HUUUUUGE day! It's the very last day of "My 31 days!" On that note, I decided to make today nice but simple. Well... It's kind of simple. I went to the dollar store and had them blow up 30 balloons for me. Blue and Black were the colors I chose. I purchased a pack of medium sized sticky labels.

On each label, I wrote different things that I love and appreciate about him. I can't stress that enough with my husband. I've mentioned several times how smart and intelligent he is. I admire the man that he is, and I always want to let him know how much he is appreciated!

I had to get him out of the house because he made it home before I did. I asked him to pick up our oldest daughter from the library. That way, I could bring the balloons in the house without him seeing me. I also asked him to stop at the store and grab me some wine and a few other items.

I figured that would occupy some of his time. He agreed to do so. Once I knew he was gone, I hurried and parked and ran everything in the apartment. Good thing our bed was already made. That was one less thing for me to worry about.

I quickly wrote on the labels, the things that I appreciate and love about him. I then stuck the labels on the balloons and I placed the balloons above the bed. I heard Dee walk through the apartment door. I finished just in time!

I opened our bedroom door with a huge smile on my face. When Dee saw the balloons, he was all dimples. I was so excited to show him what I had done. "Look babe! I wrote different things on them for you!" He began to laugh at my excitement.

His smile showed his happiness. He pulled each balloon string towards him and read each one. He hugged me for so long. He kissed my forehead and then hugged me even tighter. "Thank you sweetheart," he said, and he just held me. I can honestly say that my husband emotions were getting to him. That hug alone said so much, without him saying one word. Day 30...

Day 31- The Dance

Dark red streamers are covering the entrance into the living room. The floor is covered with black balloons and the lighting is red. Our sectional has all black throw pillows propped up. Dee walked in with a serious face, but once he noticed the décor, the look on his face seemed to change. He looked happy and calm... at ease. He saw me standing next to the couch and smiled. "Welcome to Dee's Boom Boom Room!!" I said. I could barely say that seriously. I was laughing and blushing at the same time.

"Do you like it?" I asked. As always he was all dimples. He said "I love it!" Dee's Boom boom room hunh? I thought my boom boom room would've had about 5 different bitches up in here," and he did his playful pimp laugh. Now yall know he tried it! I laughed but I couldn't turn around quick enough to punch him in his chest. "Don't play wit me Dee," I said. He laughed and rubbed his chest where I hit him. He pulled me into him and kissed my lips. Smiling he said, "I'm just playing sweetheart, all I need is you". "Yeah ok", I said with a little smirk on my face... and I gave him the side eye. I knew he was playing. I also knew that my power punch to his chest was hurting him. Ha!

Excitedly, I said "Come on!" and I pulled him to the couch to sit down. Because it was Halloween I decided to dress up. I wore a short fitted referee outfit. It was a one piece. The top of it had black and white stripes and it was attached to a short black skirt. I wore black boy shorts underneath with knee length tube socks and sneakers. I even had black lines under my eyes like the football players. I had to get into full character. I threw the remote to Dee and told him to hit play. As soon as Ciara's body party started playing, I turned into Sasha. When the music started playing, I made sure my husband didn't want to take his eyes off of me. By the look in Dee's eyes I knew he loved what he saw.

I walked through the streamers that were hanging from the ceiling. I began to dance in front of him. I danced seductively, moving my body side to side. I turned my back to him and I dipped down and slowly stood up with my butt poked out. Squats definitely helped me out with this project. I slowly turned around and we're now making eye contact. Steady dancing and swerving my hips.

My hands are caressing my inner thighs and I glide them to my outer thighs, up my stomach to my breasts, continuing to move my hips. I bit my bottom lip as he watched me. Next, I strutted right in front of him, turned around and sat down on his lap. I started to grind my lower half on his lap. His hands made their way to my hips as I was grinding on him. They go up to my breasts and he squeezed them.

I removed his hands and turned around. I crawled on top of him, with his body in between my thighs. I continued to dance. His hands are now around my waist. He glides them up and down my back and gripped my butt. He starts to smack each cheek at the same time. I wanted to laugh when I saw he had his serious face on and couldn't keep his hands off of me... I kept it cool though. I teased him really well by licking and kissing his neck and ear lobes.

We never lost eye contact, and were now face to face. Instantly, he grabbed my face and started to kiss me. He grabbed my thighs and stood up, still holding me and laid me on my back onto the couch. He was so rough. I loved it! He practically ripped my panties off. I think you all know how this ended. Needless to say, we were both breathing heavily. I smiled and said "I wasn't done dancing". He kissed my cheek, smiled and said "you were to me!" He laid on his back and pulled me on top of him. "This month has been the best month ever Joli... I love you and the love you've shown me has been remarkable. I'll never forget the things you've done for me. Thank you." "Anything for you Poppa", I said. We kissed and laid in each other's arms. Day 31....

"Lord, Thank you! There is no other like You! You are an awesome God!! I praise your name! I'm so happy right now Lord. This month has been so tiring, but you kept me strong and made it easy. My mind set is completely different when it comes to my marriage. I will continue to put you first and be the best wife to my husband that I can be. Again... I just want to say Thank You Father. In Jesus name Amen"... −*Joli Michelle*

The Afterglow

Afterglow: a happy feeling that remains after a successful or emotional event

Finally!! I accomplished 31 days of pleasing my husband! I have to say... Our marriage has done a complete 360! I'm so happy! I could never say that we don't have any arguments. This is a marriage now, come on. But we pick and choose our battles. The level of respect that we have for each other is indescribable. Our communication with each other has definitely improved. There's not a question in my mind as to him loving me. My husband by far is not an affectionate or emotional person. But he has definitely been consistent with loving me how I need him too. That's all I ever wanted. I do my best as a wife, to remain respectful, faithful and appreciative of him as well. Most of all I keep God first. If I'm upset, I have to pray before I react. Prayer is key in my marriage. I give all thanks and Glory to God for loving me unconditionally and faithfully and remaining number one in my life as well as my marriage.

-Joli Michelle

Interview with Mr. Fort

1. What day did you like most and why? *I'd say the first day, because of how excited you were about the whole thing.*

2. Do you think it improved our marriage? If so, how? *I'd say it improved our marriage. It's expected for a couple to love each other, it's like muscle memory. Sometimes you forget what it took to make it strong. I think our communication is a lot better.*

3. Could you see yourself doing the same thing for me? *I'd definitely like too, but I don't think I'd be as creative*

4. Do you think this would help couples in their relationships? *I'd say yeah it would, but as to how much it would help them? It really depends on the couple. I think overtime people naturally take each other for granted, and become quick to point out what they don't like with a tendency to forget what they have.*

5. How do you feel about me now, compared to before the 31 days? *Well I loved you then, but even more now. The 31 days really showed me what I honestly thought about you. I knew I loved you, but I didn't know how much you loved me. The 31 days really took a lot of planning. It's definitely not something you make up in 10 minutes. I now know how much you love me. I love you. Always have, always will...*

My Favorite Bible Scripture

Proverbs 31: 10-31 The Woman Who Fears the LORD

10 *t* "An excellent wife who can find?
    She is far more precious than ʲjewels.
11 The heart of her husband trusts in her,
    and he will have no lack of gain.
12 She does him good, and not harm,
    all the days of her life.
13 She ᵘseeks wool and flax,
    and works with willing hands.
14 She is like the ships of the merchant;
    she brings her food from afar.
15 She ᵃrises while it is yet night
    and ᵇprovides food for her household
    and portions for her maidens.
16 She considers a field and buys it;
with the fruit of her hands she plants a vineyard.
17 She ᵃdresses herself² with strength
    and makes her arms strong.
18 She perceives that her merchandise is profitable.
    Her lamp does not go out at night.
19 She puts her hands to the distaff,
    and her hands hold the spindle.
20 She ᵃopens her hand to ᵇthe poor
    and reaches out her hands to ᵇthe needy.
21 She is not afraid of snow for her household,
    for all her household are clothed in ᶜscarlet.⁶
22 She makes ᵈbed coverings for herself;
    her clothing is ᵉfine linen and ᶠpurple.
23 Her husband is known in ᵍthe gates
    when he sits among the elders of the land.
24 She makes ʰlinen garments and sells them;

>   she delivers sashes to the merchant.
> ²⁵ *Strength and dignity are her clothing,
>   and she laughs at the time to come.
> ²⁶ She opens her mouth with wisdom,
>   and the teaching of kindness is on her tongue.
> ²⁷ She looks well to the ways of her household
>
>   and does not eat the bread of idleness.
> ²⁸ Her children rise up and call her blessed;
>   her husband also, and he praises her:
> ²⁹ "Many ʲwomen have done ᵏexcellently,
>   but you surpass them all."
> ³⁰ ˡCharm is deceitful, and beauty is vain,
> but a woman who fears the LORD is to be praised.
> ³¹ Give her of the fruit of her hands,
>   and let her works praise her in the gates.

For reviews or comments you can email me at
jolinnichelle31days@gmail.com